Her Best F***ing Life

PLANNER & WORKBOOK

PLAN YOUR DAY, RAISE YOUR VIBE, & LIVE
YOUR BEST LIFE EVERY DAY OF YOUR LIFE

Her Best F***ing Life

PLANNER & WORKBOOK

ISBN: 1986555321
ISBN-13: 978-1986555326

Hey Girl,

I'm SO glad you're here!

Are you ready to cut out the bullshit of the day to day grind? You know, the stuff that tried to pull you down, drain you emotionally, and dim your light?

Are you ready to wake up each day feeling hopeful, inspired, on fire, and limitless? I'm talking unstoppable, can't touch this, 'on a whole new level' kind of vibes?

Are you ready to turn each and every day of your life into one that is up-leveled, upgraded, and elevated?

Are you ready to live your best f*ing life every single day of your life!?**

You came to the right place and bought the right workbook, Sister.

Use the guided planner and workbook each morning to set your intentions, show gratitude, & start your day with motivation that no-one can touch.

End each day with reflection, appreciation, and by giving yourself all the credit you deserve for getting shit done, taking no prisoners, and crushing another day of your best f***ing life.

Based off of my hit podcast "Her Best F***ing Life" on iTunes and Stitcher, this planner and workbook is a way to take the motivational, female empowering, uplifting vibes of my podcast with you every single day.

You've now got me as your coach, your personal cheerleader, & your new best girlfriend every day and at the turn of each page.

Ya'll ready for this? Lessssgo!

p.s. Share your planner and workbook pics with the hashtag #herbestfuckinglife so I can see your kickass days! Decorate it, personalize it, make it your own, and get creative!

xoxo,
Sarah

date: _____

DAILY MANTRA:

Today I will...

Wake Up Time:

I FEEL :

■ ■ ■ ■ ■ ■ ■ ■ ■ ■ ■ ■ ■ ■ ■ ■ ■ ■ ■

TODAY I AM GRATEFUL FOR:

_____

_____

_____

_____

TO DO LIST:

1.

2.

3.

4.

5.

If you have a dream, don't let anybody take it away.

SELENA QUINTANILLA-PEREZ

I practiced self love by:

_____

_____

_____

_____

♥ ♥ ♥

THINGS I ACCOMPLISHED:

1.

2.

3.

4.

5.

JOURNAL PROMPT:

What was your favorite part of today? Why?

_____

_____

_____

_____

_____

_____

Bedtime:

I FEEL :

date: _____

DAILY MANTRA:

I am available for..

Wake Up Time:

I FEEL :

■ ■ ■ ■ ■ ■ ■ ■ ■ ■ ■ ■ ■ ■ ■ ■ ■ ■ ■

TODAY I AM GRATEFUL FOR:

_____

_____

_____

_____

TO DO LIST:

1.

2.

3.

4.

5.

Say, yes, and you'll figure it out afterwards.

TINA FEY

I practiced self love by:

_____

_____

_____

_____

♥ ♥ ♥

THINGS I ACCOMPLISHED:

1.

2.

3.

4.

5.

■ ■

JOURNAL PROMPT:

What do you love about yourself?

_____

_____

_____

_____

_____

_____

Bedtime:

I FEEL :

date: _____

DAILY MANTRA:

I am able to...

TODAY I AM GRATEFUL FOR:

_____

_____

_____

_____

TO DO LIST:

1.

2.

3.

4.

5.

I can and I will. Watch me.

CARRIE GREEN

I practiced self love by:

_____

_____

_____

_____

♥ ♥ ♥

1.

2.

3.

4.

5.

■ ■ ■ ■ ■ ■ ■ ■ ■ ■ ■ ■ ■ ■ ■ ■ ■ ■

JOURNAL PROMPT:

Name one woman you admire and explain why.

_____

_____

_____

_____

_____

_____

_____

Bedtime:

I FEEL :

date: _____

DAILY MANTRA:

I believe that...

Wake Up Time:

I FEEL :

■ ■ ■ ■ ■ ■ ■ ■ ■ ■ ■ ■ ■ ■ ■ ■ ■ ■

TODAY I AM GRATEFUL FOR:

_____

_____

_____

_____

TO DO LIST:

1.

2.

3.

4.

5.

A girl should be two things: who and what she wants.

COCO CHANEL

I practiced self love by:

_____

_____

_____

_____

♥ ♥ ♥

THINGS I ACCOMPLISHED:

1.

2.

3.

4.

5.

JOURNAL PROMPT:

What are your top priorities in life?

_____

_____

_____

_____

_____

_____

_____

Bedtime:

I FEEL :

date: _____

DAILY MANTRA:

I choose to...

Wake Up Time:

I FEEL :

■ ■

TODAY I AM GRATEFUL FOR:

_____
_____
_____
_____

TO DO LIST:

1.

2.

3.

4.

5.

Both men and women should feel free to be strong.

EMMA WATSON

I practiced self love by:

_____

_____

_____

_____

♥ ♥ ♥

THINGS I ACCOMPLISHED:

1.

2.

3.

4.

5.

■ ■ ■ ■ ■ ■ ■ ■ ■ ■ ■ ■ ■ ■ ■ ■ ■ ■ ■ ■

JOURNAL PROMPT:

What was the last thing that you celebrated?

_____

_____

_____

_____

_____

_____

Bedtime:

I FEEL :

date: _____

DAILY MANTRA:

Today I will...

Wake Up Time:

I FEEL :

■ ■

TODAY I AM GRATEFUL FOR:

_____

_____

_____

_____

TO DO LIST:

1.

2.

3.

4.

5.

I believe ambition is not a dirty word, its believeing in yourself and your abilities.

REESE WITHERSPOON

I practiced self love by:

_____

_____

_____

_____

♥ ♥ ♥

1.

2.

3.

4.

5.

■ ■

JOURNAL PROMPT:

What is one thing you dream of doing?

_____

_____

_____

_____

_____

_____

_____

Bedtime:

I FEEL :

date: _____

DAILY MANTRA:

I am available for...

Wake Up Time:

I FEEL :

■ ■ ■ ■ ■ ■ ■ ■ ■ ■ ■ ■ ■ ■ ■ ■ ■ ■ ■

TODAY I AM GRATEFUL FOR:

_____

_____

_____

_____

TO DO LIST:

1.

2.

3.

4.

5.

Dreaming, after all, is a form of planning.

GLORIA STEINEM

I practiced self love by:

_____

_____

_____

_____

♥ ♥ ♥

THINGS I ACCOMPLISHED:

1.

2.

3.

4.

5.

JOURNAL PROMPT:

Describe one way you'd like to grow in the next year.

_____

_____

_____

_____

_____

_____

_____

_____

Bedtime:

I FEEL :

date: _____

DAILY MANTRA:

I am able to...

Wake Up Time:

I FEEL :

■ ■

TODAY I AM GRATEFUL FOR:

_____

_____

_____

_____

TO DO LIST:

1.

2.

3.

4.

5.

A woman becomes a force once she knows what she wants and learns how to ask for it.

CARA ALWILL LEYBA

I practiced self love by:

_____

_____

_____

_____

THINGS I ACCOMPLISHED:

1.

2.

3.

4.

5.

JOURNAL PROMPT:

How can you give yourself more time to relax?

_____

_____

_____

_____

_____

_____

Bedtime:

I FEEL :

date: _____

DAILY MANTRA:

I believe...

Wake Up Time:

I FEEL :

■ ■

TODAY I AM GRATEFUL FOR:

_____

_____

_____

_____

TO DO LIST:

1.

2.

3.

4.

5.

Nobody gets to tell you how big your dreams can be.

RACHEL HOLLIS

I practiced self love by:

_____

_____

_____

_____

♥ ♥ ♥

THINGS I ACCOMPLISHED:

1.

2.

3.

4.

5.

JOURNAL PROMPT:

What is one way you've changed in the past year?

_____

_____

_____

_____

_____

_____

_____

Bedtime:

I FEEL :

date:  _____

DAILY MANTRA:

I choose to...

Wake Up Time:

I FEEL :

▪ ▪

TODAY I AM GRATEFUL FOR:

_____

_____

_____

_____

TO DO LIST:

1.

2.

3.

4.

5.

True abundance isn't based on our net worth, it's based on our self-worth.

GABRIELLE BERNSTEIN

I practiced self love by:

_____

_____

_____

_____

♥ ♥ ♥

THINGS I ACCOMPLISHED:

1.

2.

3.

4.

5.

■ ■

JOURNAL PROMPT:

How would the people in your life describe you?

_____

_____

_____

_____

_____

_____

_____

Bedtime:

I FEEL :

date: _____

DAILY MANTRA:

Today I will...

Wake Up Time:

I FEEL :

■ ■

TODAY I AM GRATEFUL FOR:

_____

_____

_____

_____

TO DO LIST:

1.

2.

3.

4.

5.

Let nothing dim the light that shines within.

MAYA ANGELOU

I practiced self love by:

_____

_____

_____

_____

♥ ♥ ♥

1.

2.

3.

4.

5.

JOURNAL PROMPT:

What are you excited about right now?

_____

_____

_____

_____

_____

_____

_____

Bedtime:

I FEEL :

date: _____

DAILY MANTRA:

I am available for..

Wake Up Time:

I FEEL :

■ ■ ■ ■ ■ ■ ■ ■ ■ ■ ■ ■ ■ ■ ■ ■ ■ ■ ■ ■

TODAY I AM GRATEFUL FOR:

_____

_____

_____

_____

TO DO LIST:

1.

2.

3.

4.

5.

I have everything I could ever want. It just looks different than I thought.

SARAH BERGSTEIN

I practiced self love by:

_____

_____

_____

_____

♥ ♥ ♥

THINGS I ACCOMPLISHED:

1.

2.

3.

4.

5.

JOURNAL PROMPT:

What are some of your best qualities?

_____

_____

_____

_____

_____

_____

_____

Bedtime:

I FEEL :

date: _____

DAILY MANTRA:

I am able to...

Wake Up Time:

I FEEL :

■ ■ ■ ■ ■ ■ ■ ■ ■ ■ ■ ■ ■ ■ ■ ■ ■ ■ ■ ■

TODAY I AM GRATEFUL FOR:

_____

_____

_____

_____

TO DO LIST:

1.

2.

3.

4.

5.

Don't buy into the idea that women aren't strong enough to do anything they want on their own.

CHER

I practiced self love by:

_____

_____

_____

_____

♥ ♥ ♥

THINGS I ACCOMPLISHED:

1.

2.

3.

4.

5.

JOURNAL PROMPT:

What is a quote that you live by?

_____

_____

_____

_____

_____

_____

_____

Bedtime:

I FEEL :

date: _____

DAILY MANTRA:

I believe that...

Wake Up Time:

I FEEL :

■ ■

TODAY I AM GRATEFUL FOR:

_____

_____

_____

_____

TO DO LIST:

1.

2.

3.

4.

5.

The expected is what keeps us steady. It's the unexpected that changes our lives forever.

SHONDA RHIMES

I practiced self love by:

_____

_____

_____

_____

♥ ♥ ♥

THINGS I ACCOMPLISHED:

1.

2.

3.

4.

5.

■ ■ ■ ■ ■ ■ ■ ■ ■ ■ ■ ■ ■ ■ ■ ■ ■ ■ ■

JOURNAL PROMPT:

Where would your dream vacation be?

_____

_____

_____

_____

_____

_____

_____

Bedtime:

I FEEL :

date: _____

DAILY MANTRA:

I choose to...

Wake Up Time:

I FEEL :

■ ■ ■ ■ ■ ■ ■ ■ ■ ■ ■ ■ ■ ■ ■ ■ ■ ■ ■

TODAY I AM GRATEFUL FOR:

_____

_____

_____

_____

TO DO LIST:

1.

2.

3.

4.

5.

If you don't celebrate yourself, you'll settle for a life where you simply tolerate yourself.

MARSHAWN EVANS DANIELS

I practiced self love by:

_____

_____

_____

_____

♥ ♥ ♥

THINGS I ACCOMPLISHED:

1.

2.

3.

4.

5.

JOURNAL PROMPT:

What is one limiting belief that you have overcome?

_____

_____

_____

_____

_____

_____

Bedtime:

I FEEL :

date: _____

DAILY MANTRA:

Today I will...

Wake Up Time:

I FEEL :

■ ■

TODAY I AM GRATEFUL FOR:

_____

_____

_____

_____

TO DO LIST:

1.

2.

3.

4.

5.

Being authentic and honest with everyone is the best way to figure out who you are.

DEMI LOVATO

I practiced self love by:

_____

_____

_____

_____

♥ ♥ ♥

THINGS I ACCOMPLISHED:

1.

2.

3.

4.

5.

■ ■ ■ ■ ■ ■ ■ ■ ■ ■ ■ ■ ■ ■ ■ ■ ■ ■ ■

JOURNAL PROMPT:

Describe one insecurity that you have overcome.

_____

_____

_____

_____

_____

_____

_____

Bedtime:

I FEEL :

date: _____

DAILY MANTRA:

I am available for...

Wake Up Time:

I FEEL :

■ ■

TODAY I AM GRATEFUL FOR:

_____
_____
_____
_____

TO DO LIST:

1.

2.

3.

4.

5.

I'm tough, I'm ambitious, and I know exactly what i want. If that makes me a bitch, okay.

MADONNA

I practiced self love by:

_____

_____

_____

_____

♥ ♥ ♥

THINGS I ACCOMPLISHED:

1.

2.

3.

4.

5.

JOURNAL PROMPT:

Describe a time when you stood up for yourself.

_____

_____

_____

_____

_____

_____

_____

_____

Bedtime:

I FEEL :

date: _____

DAILY MANTRA:

I am able to...

Wake Up Time:

I FEEL :

■ ■

TODAY I AM GRATEFUL FOR:

_____

_____

_____

_____

TO DO LIST:

1.

2.

3.

4.

5.

The biggest adventure you can take is to live the life of your dreams.

OPRAH WINFREY

I practiced self love by:

_____

_____

_____

_____

♥ ♥ ♥

1.

2.

3.

4.

5.

■ ■ ■ ■ ■ ■ ■ ■ ■ ■ ■ ■ ■ ■ ■ ■ ■ ■ ■ ■

JOURNAL PROMPT:

If you knew you could not fail, what would you do?

_____

_____

_____

_____

_____

_____

Bedtime:

I FEEL :

date: _____

DAILY MANTRA:

I believe...

Wake Up Time:

I FEEL :

TODAY I AM GRATEFUL FOR:

_____

_____

_____

_____

TO DO LIST:

1.

2.

3.

4.

5.

If you have the courage to start, you have the courage to succeed.

MEL ROBBINS

I practiced self love by:

_____

_____

_____

_____

♥ ♥ ♥

1.

2.

3.

4.

5.

JOURNAL PROMPT:

What is your favorite form of self care?

_____

_____

_____

_____

_____

_____

_____

Bedtime:

I FEEL :

date: _____

DAILY MANTRA:

I choose to...

Wake Up Time:

I FEEL :

■ ■

TODAY I AM GRATEFUL FOR:

_____

_____

_____

_____

TO DO LIST:

1.

2.

3.

4.

5.

Being happy never goes out of style.

LILLY PULITZER

I practiced self love by:

_____

_____

_____

_____

♥ ♥ ♥

THINGS I ACCOMPLISHED:

1.

2.

3.

4.

5.

JOURNAL PROMPT:

What good have you done for those around you?

_____

_____

_____

_____

_____

_____

_____

Bedtime:

I FEEL :

date: _____

DAILY MANTRA:

Today I will...

Wake Up Time:

I FEEL :

■ ■ ■ ■ ■ ■ ■ ■ ■ ■ ■ ■ ■ ■ ■ ■ ■ ■ ■ ■

TODAY I AM GRATEFUL FOR:

_____

_____

_____

_____

TO DO LIST:

1.

2.

3.

4.

5.

Talk to yourself like you would to someone you love.
BRENE BROWN

I practiced self love by:

_____

_____

_____

_____

♥ ♥ ♥

THINGS I ACCOMPLISHED:

1.

2.

3.

4.

5.

■ ■ ■ ■ ■ ■ ■ ■ ■ ■ ■ ■ ■ ■ ■ ■ ■ ■ ■

JOURNAL PROMPT:

What is your favorite childhood memory?

_____

_____

_____

_____

_____

_____

_____

Bedtime:

I FEEL :

date: _____

DAILY MANTRA:

I am available for...

Wake Up Time:

I FEEL :

■ ■ ■ ■ ■ ■ ■ ■ ■ ■ ■ ■ ■ ■ ■ ■ ■ ■ ■

TODAY I AM GRATEFUL FOR:

_____

_____

_____

_____

TO DO LIST:

1.

2.

3.

4.

5.

Success is not about how much money you make, its about the difference you make in people's lives.
MICHELLE OBAMA

I practiced self love by:

_____

_____

_____

_____

♥ ♥ ♥

1.

2.

3.

4.

5.

■ ■ ■ ■ ■ ■ ■ ■ ■ ■ ■ ■ ■ ■ ■ ■ ■ ■ ■

JOURNAL PROMPT:

What are some of your talents that others might not know?

_____

_____

_____

_____

_____

_____

Bedtime:

I FEEL :

date: _____

Wake Up Time:

I FEEL :

TODAY I AM GRATEFUL FOR:

_____

_____

_____

_____

TO DO LIST:

1.

2.

3.

4.

5.

Character. Intelligence. Strength. Style. That makes beauty.

DIANE VON FURSTENBERG

I practiced self love by:

_____

_____

_____

_____

♥ ♥ ♥

THINGS I ACCOMPLISHED:

1.

2.

3.

4.

5.

■ ■ ■ ■ ■ ■ ■ ■ ■ ■ ■ ■ ■ ■ ■ ■ ■ ■ ■ ■

JOURNAL PROMPT:

What makes you beautiful on the inside?

_____

_____

_____

_____

_____

_____

Bedtime:

I FEEL :

date: _____

DAILY MANTRA:

I believe...

Wake Up Time:

I FEEL :

■ ■

TODAY I AM GRATEFUL FOR:

_____

_____

_____

_____

TO DO LIST:

1.

2.

3.

4.

5.

The success of every woman should be inspiration to another.

SERENA WILLIAMS

I practiced self love by:

_____

_____

_____

_____

♥ ♥ ♥

THINGS I ACCOMPLISHED:

1.

2.

3.

4.

5.

JOURNAL PROMPT:

What does your perfect day look like?

_____

_____

_____

_____

_____

_____

_____

_____

Bedtime:

I FEEL :

date: _____

DAILY MANTRA:

I choose to...

Wake Up Time:

I FEEL :

■ ■

TODAY I AM GRATEFUL FOR:

_____

_____

_____

_____

TO DO LIST:

1.

2.

3.

4.

5.

I did everything he did but backwards & in high heels.

GINGER ROGERS

I practiced self love by:

_____

_____

_____

_____

♥ ♥ ♥

THINGS I ACCOMPLISHED:

1.

2.

3.

4.

5.

JOURNAL PROMPT:

When was the last time you did something that scared you?

_____

_____

_____

_____

_____

_____

Bedtime:

I FEEL :

date: _____

DAILY MANTRA:

Today I will...

Wake Up Time:

I FEEL :

■ ■ ■ ■ ■ ■ ■ ■ ■ ■ ■ ■ ■ ■ ■ ■ ■ ■ ■

TODAY I AM GRATEFUL FOR:

_____

_____

_____

_____

TO DO LIST:

1.

2.

3.

4.

5.

How you love yourself is how you teach others to love you.

RUPI KAUR

I practiced self love by:

_____

_____

_____

_____

♥ ♥ ♥

THINGS I ACCOMPLISHED:

1.

2.

3.

4.

5.

JOURNAL PROMPT:

Describe one stereotype you have broken.

_____

_____

_____

_____

_____

_____

Bedtime:

I FEEL :

date: _____

DAILY MANTRA:

I am available for..

Wake Up Time:

I FEEL :

■ ■

TODAY I AM GRATEFUL FOR:

_____

_____

_____

_____

TO DO LIST:

1.

2.

3.

4.

5.

There are no regrets in life, just lessons.

JENNIFER ANISTON

I practiced self love by:

_____

_____

_____

_____

♥ ♥ ♥

THINGS I ACCOMPLISHED:

1.

2.

3.

4.

5.

JOURNAL PROMPT:

Who would you like to reconnect with in your life?

_____

_____

_____

_____

_____

_____

Bedtime:

I FEEL :

date: _____

DAILY MANTRA:

I am able to...

TODAY I AM GRATEFUL FOR:

_____

_____

_____

_____

TO DO LIST:

1.

2.

3.

4.

5.

I'm not frightened by anyone's perception of me.

ANGELINA JOLIE

I practiced self love by:

_____

_____

_____

_____

♥ ♥ ♥

1.

2.

3.

4.

5.

■ ■

JOURNAL PROMPT:

Where do you see yourself in 5 years?

_____

_____

_____

_____

_____

_____

Bedtime:

I FEEL :

date: _____

DAILY MANTRA:

I believe that...

Wake Up Time:

I FEEL :

■ ■

TODAY I AM GRATEFUL FOR:

_____

_____

_____

_____

TO DO LIST:

1.

2.

3.

4.

5.

If you obey all the rules, you miss all the fun.

AUDREY HEPBURN

I practiced self love by:

_____

_____

_____

_____

♥ ♥ ♥

THINGS I ACCOMPLISHED:

1.

2.

3.

4.

5.

JOURNAL PROMPT:

Where would be your dream location to live?

_____

_____

_____

_____

_____

_____

_____

Bedtime:

I FEEL :

date: _____

DAILY MANTRA:

I choose to...

Wake Up Time:

I FEEL :

■ ■

TODAY I AM GRATEFUL FOR:

_____

_____

_____

_____

TO DO LIST:

1.

2.

3.

4.

5.

I never dreamt of success. I worked for it.

ESTEE LAUDER

I practiced self love by:

_____

_____

_____

_____

♥ ♥ ♥

1.

2.

3.

4.

5.

JOURNAL PROMPT:

What would you tell your younger self?

_____

_____

_____

_____

_____

_____

Bedtime:

I FEEL :

date: _____

DAILY MANTRA:

Today I will...

Wake Up Time:

I FEEL :

■ ■

TODAY I AM GRATEFUL FOR:

_____

_____

_____

_____

TO DO LIST:

1.

2.

3.

4.

5.

The most beautiful thing you can wear is confidence.

BLAKE LIVELY

I practiced self love by:

_____

_____

_____

_____

♥ ♥ ♥

THINGS I ACCOMPLISHED:

1.

2.

3.

4.

5.

JOURNAL PROMPT:

What is one thing you would change in the world today?

_____

_____

_____

_____

_____

_____

_____

Bedtime:

I FEEL :

date: _____

DAILY MANTRA:

I am available for...

Wake Up Time:

I FEEL :

■ ■ ■ ■ ■ ■ ■ ■ ■ ■ ■ ■ ■ ■ ■ ■ ■ ■

TODAY I AM GRATEFUL FOR:

_____

_____

_____

_____

TO DO LIST:

1.

2.

3.

4.

5.

A bossy woman is someone to search out and celebrate.

AMY POEHLER

I practiced self love by:

_____

_____

_____

_____

♥ ♥ ♥

THINGS I ACCOMPLISHED:

1.

2.

3.

4.

5.

JOURNAL PROMPT:

What are you most happy about in your life?

_____

_____

_____

_____

_____

_____

Bedtime:

I FEEL :

date: _____

DAILY MANTRA:

I am able to...

Wake Up Time:

I FEEL :

■ ■ ■ ■ ■ ■ ■ ■ ■ ■ ■ ■ ■ ■ ■ ■ ■ ■ ■ ■

TODAY I AM GRATEFUL FOR:

_____

_____

_____

_____

TO DO LIST:

1.

2.

3.

4.

5.

Anytime someone tells me I can't do something, I want to do it more.

TAYLOR SWIFT

I practiced self love by:

_____

_____

_____

_____

♥ ♥ ♥

THINGS I ACCOMPLISHED:

1.

2.

3.

4.

5.

■ ■ ■ ■ ■ ■ ■ ■ ■ ■ ■ ■ ■ ■ ■ ■ ■

JOURNAL PROMPT:

Who means the world to you and why?

_____

_____

_____

_____

_____

_____

Bedtime:

I FEEL :

date: _____

DAILY MANTRA:

I believe...

Wake Up Time:

I FEEL :

■ ■ ■ ■ ■ ■ ■ ■ ■ ■ ■ ■ ■ ■ ■ ■ ■ ■ ■

TODAY I AM GRATEFUL FOR:

_____

_____

_____

_____

TO DO LIST:

1.

2.

3.

4.

5.

I may not be perfect, but I'm always me.

SELENA GOMEZ

I practiced self love by:

_____

_____

_____

_____

♥ ♥ ♥

THINGS I ACCOMPLISHED:

1.

2.

3.

4.

5.

JOURNAL PROMPT:

What does my ideal morning routine look like?

_____

_____

_____

_____

_____

_____

_____

Bedtime:

I FEEL :

date: _____

DAILY MANTRA:

I choose to...

Wake Up Time:

I FEEL :

■ ■ ■ ■ ■ ■ ■ ■ ■ ■ ■ ■ ■ ■ ■ ■ ■ ■ ■

TODAY I AM GRATEFUL FOR:

_____

_____

_____

_____

TO DO LIST:

1.

2.

3.

4.

5.

Do not live someone else's life and someone else's idea of what womanhood is.

VIOLA DAVIS

I practiced self love by:

_____

_____

_____

_____

♥ ♥ ♥

THINGS I ACCOMPLISHED:

1.

2.

3.

4.

5.

JOURNAL PROMPT:

What makes you proud to be a woman?

_____

_____

_____

_____

_____

_____

Bedtime:

I FEEL :

date: _____

DAILY MANTRA:

Today I will...

Wake Up Time:

I FEEL :

■ ■ ■ ■ ■ ■ ■ ■ ■ ■ ■ ■ ■ ■ ■ ■ ■ ■

TODAY I AM GRATEFUL FOR:

_____

_____

_____

_____

TO DO LIST:

1.

2.

3.

4.

5.

Love yourself first and everything else falls into line.

LUCILLE BALL

I practiced self love by:

_____

_____

_____

_____

♥ ♥ ♥

THINGS I ACCOMPLISHED:

1.

2.

3.

4.

5.

JOURNAL PROMPT:

What is something new that you would love to learn?

_____

_____

_____

_____

_____

_____

Bedtime:

I FEEL :

date: _____

DAILY MANTRA:

I am available for...

Wake Up Time:

I FEEL :

TODAY I AM GRATEFUL FOR:

_____

_____

_____

_____

TO DO LIST:

1.

2.

3.

4.

5.

It's never too late-never too late to start over, never too late to be happy.

JANE FONDA

I practiced self love by:

_____

_____

_____

_____

♥ ♥ ♥

THINGS I ACCOMPLISHED:

1.

2.

3.

4.

5.

JOURNAL PROMPT:

If you won $10,000 what would you do with it?

_____

_____

_____

_____

_____

_____

Bedtime:

I FEEL :

date: _____

DAILY MANTRA:

I am able to...

Wake Up Time:

I FEEL :

■ ■

TODAY I AM GRATEFUL FOR:

_____

_____

_____

_____

TO DO LIST:

1.

2.

3.

4.

5.

Style is a way to say who you are without having to speak.

RACHEL ZOE

I practiced self love by:

_____

_____

_____

_____

♥ ♥ ♥

1.

2.

3.

4.

5.

■ ■

JOURNAL PROMPT:

Name one woman in history you'd love to speak with.

_____

_____

_____

_____

_____

_____

_____

Bedtime:

I FEEL :

date: _____

DAILY MANTRA:

I believe...

Wake Up Time:

I FEEL :

■ ■

TODAY I AM GRATEFUL FOR:

_____

_____

_____

_____

TO DO LIST:

1.

2.

3.

4.

5.

Force it into your brain. You're a badass and you deserve to be here.

GIGI HADID

I practiced self love by:

_____

_____

_____

_____

♥ ♥ ♥

THINGS I ACCOMPLISHED:

1.

2.

3.

4.

5.

■ ■ ■ ■ ■ ■ ■ ■ ■ ■ ■ ■ ■ ■ ■ ■ ■ ■

JOURNAL PROMPT:

Describe your perfect day off.

_____

_____

_____

_____

_____

_____

_____

Bedtime:

I FEEL :

date: _____

DAILY MANTRA:

I choose to...

Wake Up Time:

I FEEL :

TODAY I AM GRATEFUL FOR:

_____

_____

_____

_____

TO DO LIST:

1.

2.

3.

4.

5.

Everything has beauty but not everyone sees it.

JENNIFER LAWRENCE

I practiced self love by:

_____

_____

_____

_____

♥ ♥ ♥

THINGS I ACCOMPLISHED:

1.

2.

3.

4.

5.

JOURNAL PROMPT:

What was the last amazing book you read?

_____

_____

_____

_____

_____

_____

Bedtime:

I FEEL :

date: _____

DAILY MANTRA:

Today I will...

Wake Up Time:

I FEEL :

- -

TODAY I AM GRATEFUL FOR:

_____

_____

_____

_____

TO DO LIST:

1.

2.

3.

4.

5.

You don't know how strong you are until you have to be.

LEA MICHELLE

I practiced self love by:

_____

_____

_____

_____

♥ ♥ ♥

THINGS I ACCOMPLISHED:

1.

2.

3.

4.

5.

JOURNAL PROMPT:

One thing I'll never regret is...

_____

_____

_____

_____

_____

_____

_____

Bedtime:

I FEEL :

date: _____

DAILY MANTRA:

I am available for..

TODAY I AM GRATEFUL FOR:

_____

_____

_____

_____

TO DO LIST:

1.

2.

3.

4.

5.

If you don't love yourself, you can't love anybody else.

JENNIFER LOPEZ

I practiced self love by:

_____

_____

_____

_____

♥ ♥ ♥

THINGS I ACCOMPLISHED:

1.

2.

3.

4.

5.

■ ■ ■ ■ ■ ■ ■ ■ ■ ■ ■ ■ ■ ■ ■ ■ ■ ■ ■ ■

JOURNAL PROMPT:

What is a valuable lesson you've learned in life?

_____

_____

_____

_____

_____

_____

Bedtime:

I FEEL :

date: _____

DAILY MANTRA:

I am able to...

Wake Up Time:

I FEEL :

■ ■

TODAY I AM GRATEFUL FOR:

_____

_____

_____

_____

TO DO LIST:

1.

2.

3.

4.

5.

Pour yourself a drink, put some lipstick on, and pull yourself together.

ELIZABETH TAYLOR

I practiced self love by:

_____

_____

_____

_____

♥ ♥ ♥

1.

2.

3.

4.

5.

■ ■ ■ ■ ■ ■ ■ ■ ■ ■ ■ ■ ■ ■ ■ ■ ■ ■ ■

JOURNAL PROMPT:

What was your biggest victory today?

_____

_____

_____

_____

_____

_____

Bedtime:

I FEEL :

date: _____

DAILY MANTRA:

I believe that...

Wake Up Time:

I FEEL :

■ ■

TODAY I AM GRATEFUL FOR:

_____

_____

_____

_____

TO DO LIST:

1.

2.

3.

4.

5.

You are allowed to be both a masterpiece and a work in progress simultaneously.

SOPHIA BUSH

I practiced self love by:

_____

_____

_____

_____

♥ ♥ ♥

THINGS I ACCOMPLISHED:

1.

2.

3.

4.

5.

JOURNAL PROMPT:

What is your favorite way to relax?

_____

_____

_____

_____

_____

_____

_____

Bedtime:

I FEEL :

date: _____

DAILY MANTRA:

I choose to...

Wake Up Time:

I FEEL :

■ ■

TODAY I AM GRATEFUL FOR:

_____
_____
_____
_____

TO DO LIST:

1.

2.

3.

4.

5.

Find out who you are and be that person.

ELLEN DEGENERES

I practiced self love by:

_____

_____

_____

_____

♥ ♥ ♥

1.

2.

3.

4.

5.

JOURNAL PROMPT:

If you had one wish granted, what would it be?

_____

_____

_____

_____

_____

_____

_____

Bedtime:

I FEEL :

date: _____

DAILY MANTRA:

Today I will...

Wake Up Time:

I FEEL :

■ ■

TODAY I AM GRATEFUL FOR:

_____

_____

_____

_____

TO DO LIST:

1.

2.

3.

4.

5.

It is better to live your own destiny imperfectly than to live an imitation of someone else's perfectly.
ELIZABETH GILBERT

I practiced self love by:

_____

_____

_____

_____

♥ ♥ ♥

THINGS I ACCOMPLISHED:

1.

2.

3.

4.

5.

JOURNAL PROMPT:

What is on your to do list that doesn't need to be?

_____

_____

_____

_____

_____

_____

Bedtime:

I FEEL :

date: _____

DAILY MANTRA:

I am available for...

Wake Up Time:

I FEEL :

■ ■ ■ ■ ■ ■ ■ ■ ■ ■ ■ ■ ■ ■ ■ ■ ■ ■ ■

TODAY I AM GRATEFUL FOR:

_____

_____

_____

_____

TO DO LIST:

1.

2.

3.

4.

5.

You must never be fearful about what you are doing when it is right.

ROSA PARKS

I practiced self love by:

_____

_____

_____

_____

♥ ♥ ♥

THINGS I ACCOMPLISHED:

1.

2.

3.

4.

5.

JOURNAL PROMPT:

What do you want people to know about you?

_____

_____

_____

_____

_____

Bedtime:

I FEEL :

date: _____

DAILY MANTRA:

I am able to...

Wake Up Time:

I FEEL :

■ ■

TODAY I AM GRATEFUL FOR:

_____

_____

_____

_____

TO DO LIST:

1.

2.

3.

4.

5.

I am not afraid of storms, for I am learning how to sail my ship.

LOUISA MAY ALCOTT

I practiced self love by:

_____

_____

_____

_____

♥ ♥ ♥

THINGS I ACCOMPLISHED:

1.

2.

3.

4.

5.

JOURNAL PROMPT:

Describe your day with one word.

_____

_____

_____

_____

_____

_____

_____

Bedtime:

I FEEL :

date: _____

DAILY MANTRA:

I believe...

Wake Up Time:

I FEEL :

TODAY I AM GRATEFUL FOR:

_____

_____

_____

_____

TO DO LIST:

1.

2.

3.

4.

5.

It took me quite a long time to develop a voice, and now that I have it, I am not going to be silent.

MADELEINE ALBRIGHT

I practiced self love by:

_____

_____

_____

_____

♥ ♥ ♥

THINGS I ACCOMPLISHED:

1.

2.

3.

4.

5.

JOURNAL PROMPT:

What do you want to let go of in your life?

_____

_____

_____

_____

_____

_____

Bedtime:

I FEEL :

date: _____

DAILY MANTRA:

I choose to...

Wake Up Time:

I FEEL :

■ ■

TODAY I AM GRATEFUL FOR:

_____

_____

_____

_____

TO DO LIST:

1.

2.

3.

4.

5.

I am my own muse. The subject I know best. The subject I want to better.

FRIDA KAHLO

I practiced self love by:

_____

_____

_____

_____

♥ ♥ ♥

1.

2.

3.

4.

5.

JOURNAL PROMPT:

What do you need to heal in your life?

_____

_____

_____

_____

_____

_____

_____

Bedtime:

I FEEL :

date: _____

DAILY MANTRA:

Today I will...

Wake Up Time:

I FEEL :

■ ■

TODAY I AM GRATEFUL FOR:

TO DO LIST:

_____

1.

_____

2.

_____

3.

_____

4.

Only do what your heart tells you.

5.

PRINCESS DIANA

I practiced self love by:

_____

_____

_____

_____

♥ ♥ ♥

THINGS I ACCOMPLISHED:

1.

2.

3.

4.

5.

JOURNAL PROMPT:

What makes you feel truly alive?

_____

_____

_____

_____

_____

_____

_____

Bedtime:

I FEEL :

date: _____

DAILY MANTRA:

I am available for...

Wake Up Time:

I FEEL :

■ ■

TODAY I AM GRATEFUL FOR:

_____

_____

_____

_____

TO DO LIST:

1.

2.

3.

4.

5.

Compete with yourself, not with others.

SOPHIA AMORUSO

I practiced self love by:

_____

_____

_____

_____

♥ ♥ ♥

THINGS I ACCOMPLISHED:

1.

2.

3.

4.

5.

JOURNAL PROMPT:

What is your top goal in life right now?

_____

_____

_____

_____

_____

_____

_____

Bedtime:

I FEEL :

date: _____

DAILY MANTRA:

I am able to...

Wake Up Time:

I FEEL :

■ ■ ■ ■ ■ ■ ■ ■ ■ ■ ■ ■ ■ ■ ■ ■ ■ ■ ■ ■

TODAY I AM GRATEFUL FOR:

_____

_____

_____

_____

TO DO LIST:

1.

2.

3.

4.

5.

I can't think of any better representation of beauty than someone who is unafraid to be herself.
EMMA STONE

I practiced self love by:

_____

_____

_____

_____

♥ ♥ ♥

THINGS I ACCOMPLISHED:

1.

2.

3.

4.

5.

JOURNAL PROMPT:

If you wrote a book about your life, what would its title be?

_____

_____

_____

_____

_____

_____

_____

Bedtime:

I FEEL :

date: _____

DAILY MANTRA:

I believe...

Wake Up Time:

I FEEL :

■ ■

TODAY I AM GRATEFUL FOR:

TO DO LIST:

_____

_____

_____

_____

1.

2.

3.

4.

5.

People respond well to those that are sure of what they want.

ANNA WINTOUR

I practiced self love by:

_____

_____

_____

_____

♥ ♥ ♥

THINGS I ACCOMPLISHED:

1.

2.

3.

4.

5.

JOURNAL PROMPT:

Name the people in your life that make you feel loved.

_____

_____

_____

_____

_____

_____

_____

_____

Bedtime:

I FEEL :

date: _____

DAILY MANTRA:

I choose to...

Wake Up Time:

I FEEL :

■ ■

TODAY I AM GRATEFUL FOR:

_____

_____

_____

_____

TO DO LIST:

1.

2.

3.

4.

5.

The most common way people give up their power is by thinking they don't have any.
ALICE WALKER

I practiced self love by:

_____

_____

_____

_____

♥ ♥ ♥

THINGS I ACCOMPLISHED:

1.

2.

3.

4.

5.

JOURNAL PROMPT:

What life lesson have you learned from a movie?

_____

_____

_____

_____

_____

_____

_____

Bedtime:

I FEEL :

date: _____

DAILY MANTRA:

Today I will...

Wake Up Time:

I FEEL :

■ ■

TODAY I AM GRATEFUL FOR:

_____

_____

_____

_____

TO DO LIST:

1.

2.

3.

4.

5.

Power is not given to you. You have to take it.

BEYONCE KNOWLES

I practiced self love by:

_____

_____

_____

_____

♥ ♥ ♥

THINGS I ACCOMPLISHED:

1.

2.

3.

4.

5.

JOURNAL PROMPT:

What would you like to spend more time doing?

_____

_____

_____

_____

_____

_____

Bedtime:

I FEEL :

date: _____

DAILY MANTRA:

I am available for..

Wake Up Time:

I FEEL :

■ ■ ■ ■ ■ ■ ■ ■ ■ ■ ■ ■ ■ ■ ■ ■ ■ ■ ■

TODAY I AM GRATEFUL FOR:

_____

_____

_____

_____

TO DO LIST:

1.

2.

3.

4.

5.

People will chronically underestimate you. Let that be your fuel.
MELODY MOEZZI

I practiced self love by:

_____

_____

_____

_____

♥ ♥ ♥

THINGS I ACCOMPLISHED:

1.

2.

3.

4.

5.

JOURNAL PROMPT:

What is the best gift you have ever received?

_____

_____

_____

_____

_____

_____

_____

Bedtime:

I FEEL :

date: _____

I am able to...

Wake Up Time:

I FEEL :

TODAY I AM GRATEFUL FOR:

_____

_____

_____

_____

TO DO LIST:

1.

2.

3.

4.

5.

Buckle up and know that it's going to be a tremendous amount of work, But embrace it.

TORY BURCH

I practiced self love by:

_____

_____

_____

_____

♥ ♥ ♥

1.

2.

3.

4.

5.

■ ■ ■ ■ ■ ■ ■ ■ ■ ■ ■ ■ ■ ■ ■ ■ ■ ■

JOURNAL PROMPT:

What has been your biggest breakthrough lately?

_____

_____

_____

_____

_____

_____

Bedtime:

I FEEL :

date: _____

I believe that...

Wake Up Time:

I FEEL :

■ ■

TODAY I AM GRATEFUL FOR:

_____

_____

_____

_____

TO DO LIST:

1.

2.

3.

4.

5.

Put your ear down close to your soul and listen hard.

ANNE SEXTON

I practiced self love by:

_____

_____

_____

_____

♥ ♥ ♥

THINGS I ACCOMPLISHED:

1.

2.

3.

4.

5.

JOURNAL PROMPT:

What could you upgrade about your day to make it better?

_____

_____

_____

_____

_____

_____

_____

Bedtime:

I FEEL :

date: _____

DAILY MANTRA:

I choose to...

Wake Up Time:

I FEEL :

■ ■ ■ ■ ■ ■ ■ ■ ■ ■ ■ ■ ■ ■ ■ ■ ■ ■ ■

TODAY I AM GRATEFUL FOR:

_____

_____

_____

_____

TO DO LIST:

1.

2.

3.

4.

5.

Each and every one of us was created on purpose and for a purpose.

SARAH ORDO

I practiced self love by:

_____

_____

_____

_____

♥ ♥ ♥

THINGS I ACCOMPLISHED:

1.

2.

3.

4.

5.

JOURNAL PROMPT:

What makes you, YOU?

_____

_____

_____

_____

_____

_____

Bedtime:

I FEEL :

About The Author

As an entrepreneur, makeup artist, YouTuber, podcast host, and blogger, Sarah Ordo is your not-so-average female millennial craving to leave her mark on this world in more ways than one. Her award-winning on location hair and makeup company (based out of Metro Detroit), 24Luxe Hair & Makeup, has been making clients and brides look stunning for their special occasions since 2013. Her YouTube channel and Instagram page reach thousands of her followers daily featuring a variety of beauty, health, lifestyle, and wellness posts and videos. Her Youtube videos documenting and following her sobriety have reached thousands of viewers internationally, and have even been featured on Dateline NBC.

Sarah has been featured on and interviewed for numerous blogs and podcasts including Cara Alwill Leyba's Style Your Mind Podcast, Courtney Bentley's Fit Fierce & Fabulous Podcast, and the Soul In The Raw Podcast. On her website, sarahordo.com, Sarah blogs about living sober, self-love, mental health, and many other raw, honest topics. She also features reviews of the newest beauty, health, & lifestyle products and trends.

Sober as F✳✳✳ is the first full-length memoir and book written by Sarah, which was released in May 2017. Innerbloom is her second full-length book, which is a personal development/memoir hybrid released in December 2017, following how she rebuilt her life during her journey in sobriety and beyond. Sober as F✳✳✳:The Workbook is an interactive workbook and journal based off of her original memoir. Her Best F✳✳✳ing Life Planner & Workbook was created for her podcast audience to be a creative, fun way for women to plan each day with intention and a positive vibe.

Follow Sarah: www.sarahordo.com
Youtube: Sarah Ordo
Instagram: @24Luxe_Sarah
Podcast: Her Best F✳✳✳ing Life on iTunes & Stitcher

Made in the USA
Monee, IL
14 November 2019